DAVID

INTRODUCTION

David Colman Rose was born in London on 30 January 1957. He attended City of London School and studied law at the University of Leeds and Queens Mary's College, London. He travelled extensively, was a keen sportsman and musician until the onset of cancer, revealed in a biopsy on 30 January 1977. He died in London on 5 July 1978.

DAVID

Of the previously published *Journey into Immortality* by Aubrey Rose (Lennard Publishing, 1997), various compliments were paid:

> *I don't think I have ever read a book with such an incredible sense of immediacy. You have written with great inspiration. When I finished the book I felt very sorry indeed never to have known David.*
>
> Sir Martin Gilbert CBE, official biographer of Sir Winston Churchill

> *If this is the quality of which human beings may be made, then humanity is indeed worth saving. Read on and you will derive strength and belief from this book.*
>
> Martyn Goff OBE, former chairman, Book Trust and administrator of the Booker Prize

> *I read through your amazing book at almost one gulp. A lovely tribute to your son. I wish I had known him.*
>
> Barbara Griggs, author and journalist

> *I read it from beginning to end in one session simply because I could not put it down. Beautifully written, with great tenderness and love.*
>
> Anne Ranasinghe, author and poet

INTRODUCTION

The work is unique for so many reasons. To say that it is deeply moving is an understatement. There emerged a beauty that seemed to transcend grief.

Erich Segal, author of *Love Story*. Celebrated novelist and academic

You have put it together beautifully. There is something noble and sublime in this story. Your book is like a lamp shining as a beacon. Uplifting, a beautiful book.

Dr L.M. Singhvi, Indian High Commissioner

To write such a book is a moving and splendid thing to have done.

Rt. Hon. Lord Carr of Hadley, former Home Secretary

Sections of ***Journey into Immortality*** are reproduced here, by kind permission of Lennard Publishing.

HOME AGAIN

In May 1987 David returned to the family home, not to Highgate, but to Hadley Green, a pleasant semi-rural spot on the edge of north London where the countryside begins, to which we had moved five-and-a-half years before. The house was an old one, dating from 1767. We had fallen in love with its garden, its massive Cedars of Lebanon, banks of rhododendrons and azaleas, profusion of roses, old well and thatched summer house. We bought the garden, and the house came too.

The purchase transaction likewise had something of an old-world character. The owner, a former Cabinet Minister, one of that rare breed who, despite a career in politics, remained upright and respected, shook hands with me to confirm the transaction. That handshake we regarded as binding on us both. The legal documents were a technical addendum.

In 1984 he had agreed to open an exhibition of David's works, poems and drawings, as well as tapestries and pottery based on those drawings and designs, at the Barnet Art Centre, a flourishing home of the arts housed in The Old Bull building in Barnet, close to our home. At the same time, Dame Cicely Saunders came to talk at a public meeting linked to the exhibition on the growing hospice movement in Britain of which she had been the principal pioneer.

The exhibition raised a goodly sum for cancer research, as also had a previous exhibition of David's work held in the Ben Uri Art Gallery in London's West End in September 1983, opened on that occasion by Greville Janner QC MP, a good friend, and the then lay leader of British Jews.

Despite his death, David continued, in the eyes of many, to live on in his works. To us, he lived on in reality.

His strange, colourful drawings intrigued and fascinated people.

One of them, Roman Halter, distinguished in design, sculpture and the creation of striking stained-glass windows, was drawn to David through these patterns.

In his own time, and refusing to accept payment, he mounted the exhibition, in wood and perspex, designing, cutting, framing, so that we could, with pride, and gratitude to him, survey in the exhibition halls Roman's own singular tribute to a fellow artist.

In 1987, for the first time, we had confirmation from David himself of the significance of the colours and shapes. Leslie Flint, who had been faithfully assisted in much of his career by his secretary, Bram Rogers, came one bright May day to our home with Bram and others in the small group, and held a sitting in our dining room. The old, original, wooden shutters of the house came into practical use, possibly for the first time this century, in helping to keep out the sunlight.

David was delighted with the way his mother had reproduced his drawings in tapestry and needlework. *'Better than my originals,*' he commented. He went on at some length to explain the origin of his designs:

> *'In their own way the pictures had meaning. Each motif represents experiences. When I was lying there my mind was transported, received visions and imprints. I tried to recreate things. They represent more than they seem. Each part represents aspects of emotion and feeling, not just myself. There is a link.*
>
> *They are symbolic to a point, but represent individuals, emotions. I realise now someone was guiding me. I have met people here who were creative and artistic in their own time. I was much influenced by Barney. There is a collective harmony. They tell a story. there is much more to it than meets the eye. I didn't know it at the time. I knew I didn't have long to stay with you. The way was being prepared for me. I was doing that to express things I didn't understand.*
>
> *Since I've been here, I've met people and understand they were utilising me in a special way.*
>
> *I love you. I shall always be behind you, every step of the way. There are people here you never mentioned. We are a much bigger, wider family. We are all one. I shall remain for a long time the individual as you remember me, although I shall be on a much different level in some respects.*
>
> *People are being prepared. We are never alone. In the nights, when I didn't sleep, I was not alone. Nothing can separate us. We are much bigger than we seem. I knew that I had a death*

warrant. It didn't worry me. I was worried about you. The things I might have done I can do here. Everything here is much more real than you will ever know.

We are like brothers and sisters, much more than that. We are not that far away as you may think. Time for us is not as it is for you. We are a family, a much bigger family than you can imagine. Some have been here for centuries. Never grieve for me. I love you.'

David's words flowed clearly, unhesitatingly, with such a sense of affection and attachment. I reproduce here only extracts. He was now here with us at home, not merely a sense of his presence, but his very words. We detected the faintest wistfulness at his not being here physically too. But we knew the strength of the link that could never be broken, providing a confidence and an assurance that has sustained me ever since his death, and has enabled me to cope with his passing from us.

In July 1989, our daughter Esther married. Both ceremony and celebration took place in the beautiful garden at Monkenholt, the name of our house. Numerous guests commented on the singularly happy atmosphere. Weeks later we held one of our rare sittings with Leslie Flint in his retirement home on the South coast. David spoke to us. He commented that he, and others of the family with him, had been present and shared greatly in our joy. Mickey, ever jovial, added that he had also been present, adding, *'You had many more guests there than you imagined'*. I responded that at least I did not have to pay for the unseen guests.

In all the messages I have heard, and those transcribed in book form, especially of the remarkable communicator known as Silver Birch, I have never failed to be impressed by their constant, crystal-clear clarity of expression, their absence of ambiguity or imprecision. In like manner I feel that if there is one single sentence in this book that is not immediately apparent to the reader as to its sense and purport, then I will have failed in what I have set out to achieve. Words are given to us to explain, to clarify, to inform; not to confuse.

As with all our sittings with Leslie Flint, elements of humour and fun were never far away. Mickey liked our new home. *'It's smashing and loaded with people,'* he said, referring to past occupants, including one by name. Suddenly out of the blue, linked to no one present or to our home, emerged the rather superior accent of one who gave her name in full and with distinctiveness.

'I am Sarah Ann Goodwin. What an interesting young man [David]. Very talented, artistic, creative. When I was on your side, I had no idea of communication. I thought when you were dead, you'd had it.'

She described herself as a friend of the artist Laura Knight, and also of Lady Conan Doyle. *'She was interested in this spiritual thing. I didn't fall for that, but I've got no alternative now.'*

She referred to her marriage and living in Derby. She obviously disliked both place and status. When asked if she had been one of the women who, in Suffragette times, had chained themselves railings, she replied, *'Good God, no. It was bad enough chained to a man, let alone railings.'*

Her rather precise accent reminded me somewhat of the tones of Lilian Bayliss, a former director of the celebrated Old Vic Theatre in London, who, at a previous sitting, had compared her reign as director with the current drama performed at that establishment.

In referring to the continuation of this Oxford-type English pronunciation, Mickey, the perennial Cockney gamin, reminded us that some people continued to be caught up in class memories. *'Those sorts of people used to put it on. It took time to change and adjust,'* he added.

The theatre, and the world of music and entertainment, where words and sounds are of significance, featured prominently in both messages and sessions, among communicators and sitters alike. The level of the messages, the sittings, varied likewise from the mundane, the personal, the prosaic, to the humorous, even hilarious, on to sublime realms of philosophy, truth and inspiration.

There is so much that remains to be written and to be investigated: the thought forces that create speech; the messages from all ages and races; the wonderful universal laws that emerge from the hundreds of communications I have heard and read; the centrality of love in everything; the very real problems of the orthodox and conforming of all religions and anti-religions on being translated to the spirit world; the light thrown on events, historical, political, personal, and social, of the past and the present; the vital evidence of the messages; the constant progression of souls based on their spirituality, the planets and the galaxies and their occupants; the relativity of the space-time dimension, and also the reality of further dimensions, a matter David had written about when just 13 years of age.

All these things remain to be considered, and understood, and set out clearly, and must become the basis of the crucial changes that are ahead of us in the brief remainder of this century, and in the next century, if the human race is to survive. Central to everything is the sacredness of life, the unity of vibration and of essence that pervades all things.

Apart from the messages through mediumship, there is, in this latter half of the 20th century, increasing evidence and acknowledgement of other forms of spiritual presence, in healing certainly, in the understanding of reincarnation, in materialisation, in automatic writing, in psychic painting and photography, and in the real effect on material substances of mental and non-physical processes. Not all that is said or claimed is genuine or accurate, but a sound body of evidence remains to warrant credence and persistent and scientific investigation.

Many who pass on find they link together with individuals or groups of like spirit and inclination, often traversing previous marriage or family ties, but usually continuing intellectual and creative interests at the stage left off at death. People continue to grow in the spirit world. One of the most inspiring communications came from Sir Arthur Conan Doyle, who died in 1930. It is almost unfair to quote any extract in part, but a few passages deserve mention.

'Within us lies an inmost centre of our being, a divine birthplace of man's spirit, which even to reach, much less to comprehend. is beyond all intellectual striving of attainment. If a man attempts to reach this power by intellect alone, without due attunement, without growth of the spirit, there must inevitably be disaster. Yet if that same man will strive with mind and heart and spirit to seek the kingdom, holding fast in simple and childlike faith, he must reach that plane of the universal and there receive truth and power and life from the font of all life.'

He mentions reasons 'which make it impossible for the finite mind ever to comprehend eternity', and comments in words akin to the Hindu and Buddhist traditions: *'Again we can only help you by suggesting that eternity is best represented by the great wheel which is never checked, never halted on its course.'*

As a former doctor he comments: *'Until medicine deigns to study the laws governing man's spiritual being it will continue – confronted and baffled by obscure diseases.'* Finally: *'It is profoundly difficult to express spiritual realities with words fitted only to describe material and physical conditions. Nevertheless, I would hold out to all people a hope beautiful and true beyond compare. I would describe a life perfect in its power to express all the higher feelings and attributes which lie hidden in the depths of man's nature. Not one soul, whether it be of a white, a black, a yellow or a red man, but finds provision made for it in the vast universe of the spirit. Were the words mine I would show a world of spirit ever evolving, opening to new vista after vista of beauty. As one attains one sees fresh heights beyond. The air grows finer, brighter. Exultation fills one's being, nerving one to fresh effort and attainment.'*

Everything I learned from my study of the world of the spirit has very real consequences for the ordering of society. It will take many generations before those consequences are given practical effect. To transfer into daily reality lessons which many will not, cannot, accept will require a new kind of leadership, suitable for a new age; men and women of a very special and rare quality. It is a quality that combines a profound spiritual belief with an ability to deal with political and economic realities and details. Human affairs may well sink into far darker chasms before such leaders of light emerge.

But for us, as a family, as for all families, we continued our daily pattern, far removed from the lofty heights described by Conan Doyle. Each day brings urgent practical problems, economic and social needs and pressures. If we could relate each day to a background of centuries, perceive that each material step has a non-material significance. If, above all, we are able to survey our limited years here within a wider context of a life that changes, but does not end, with death, it may be that we will gradually, haltingly, begin to evaporate the hatred and prejudice and violence that renews itself continually in our world.

For us, as a family, we know that the death of one of us is not the end of the family, only a change, that reunion, partially achieved through the messages, will take place in the reality beyond. This understanding is part of the impact of David on our lives, our thoughts, and our beliefs.

CREATIVE TALENT – POEMS

George Lamming

In 1980 the University of the West Indies bestowed an Honorary Doctorate of Literature on George Lamming in recognition of his important work over several decades in writing about life in the Caribbean. Prior to this he received the Somerset Maugham Award for Literature, a Canadian Council Fellowship, and a Guggenheim Fellowship to the USA.

He was born in the small but beautiful West Indian island of Barbados, described graphically in his famous novel *In the Castle of my Skin.* He has lived in England and also spends much of his time in the United States as a visiting lecturer at a number of universities.

George Lamming's novels are highly regarded as part of the modern literature of the Caribbean and are in demand in many parts of the world. His native Barbados, where he spent much of his time, has honoured him for his contribution to its culture.

DAVID

Appreciation

I met David for the first time after his death. One summer evening, with the roses wilting out front and a moderate sunlight everywhere, I had followed his father into the Highgate house, and later up the stairs and through a wilderness of family rooms. These were not in use. Half a home had been uninhabitable by recent flood. We were inspecting damage; talked about the erratic ways of the building trade, the anxiety of living in this private state of emergency, the strain of waiting for old, familiar comforts to come back.

There is, perhaps, no way to explain how, in so short a time, the name, David, had become a living presence, how this translation of world into feeling had left its signature on every observation we made. But this had happened to me before I started down the stairs to be introduced into the family circle.

They were in the living room, now cosy and crowded with things; favourite pieces of furniture, photograph albums, all the emblems of strong family feeling. And suddenly I saw the small pile of pictures. These were David, his paintings, which in a moment had startled me into a strange recognition of his meaning for those who had survived him. This brilliant geometry of visions and dreams started in my mind a music of ancient galaxies, modern cathedrals of stained glass, a curious marriage of Now and Eternity in startling raiment. An infinite glory of colours!

There is an interval of seven years and more between those visions and the quiet, melancholy reflections of a boy who was in the habit of looking closely at what he saw. Nature had claimed him, and he perceived with a feeling eye.

CREATIVE TALENT – POEMS

Poetry is a way of ordering feeling and making it known through language that is memorable. If the reader begins as a stranger, the poem sooner or later converts you into an intimate who can claim the poet's experience as your own.

The poem may begin from a quite uneventful circumstance, like watching, casually at first, a television account of a country far away. Such is the case with his poem, 'Drought'. There is more to the title than a literal failure of rain. And it is the way David orders his experience of seeing the television image that makes the other meaning of drought strike home:

> *The people ask for rain*
> *The children pray for rain*
> *Old women cry for rain*

The plea is repeated three times, but in a descending order of hope. The collective expectation of 'the people' soon gives way to the implied terror of children on their knees, and settles finally in a cry of resignation from old women, the most fragile and vulnerable of all.

> *Cows' bones show through their thigh*
> *Men in hell's dirt do lie.*

It is a stark image of slow dying, of crucifixion by nature, which may have registered on him as the sad condition of India, even without the affliction of drought. The occasional infelicities of the verse are negligible beside this gift of the feeling eye and the inner ear. And it seems to me quite remarkable in one so young.

But I have also been struck by the way he was learning to create out of a simple domestic occurrence, like the gift of a toy gun, a metaphor for a larger and truly tragic human aberration. The reality of violence, the sport of killing, achieves a horror all the more sickening when it is equated with something as apparently harmless as 'a funny clicking sound':

> *My people gave me a toy*
> *And warned me it was wild*
> *But I did not understand*
> *What it could do to boy and man*
> *It made a funny clicking sound*

It is impossible to say where this way with words would have taken him. The lyrics he wrote later are evidence of a growing social consciousness.

There is a note of bitter regret when he sings about the abuse of power by some idle, suburban bureaucrat, and the anger is never far from the surface when he reports on the pleasures men imagine they derive from the exploitation of the female body.

If David continues to dominate the thought and conversation of his family and friends, it is because his courage in death had made them all the more aware of the fact that he brought to their ordinary affections a quality that is rare. He was specially blessed with the gift of moral feeling.

HIS POEMS

From an early age, David had an instinct for poetry, not so much in reading, but rather the creation of poems. A few were written in response to school projects, others stimulated by his own natural feelings.

The first poem was written when David was eight or nine, the remainder when aged 13 or 14.

HIS POEMS

The Blackbird

A blackbird sitting in a tree
Sings his song of melody.
He sings his song so loud and clear,
So all the people round can hear.

But the people hurrying by
Do not hear the bird on high.
They are too busy with other things,
To hear the song the blackbird sings.

But the blackbird does not care
About the people hurrying there.
He sings his song himself to please,
Sitting there amongst the trees.

DAVID

Humans v Nature

All is quiet, all is still,
The trees have leaves,
The grass and hill
Do not make a noisy sound
Until the day men came around.

Black smoke so early in the day,
That all the day is turned away,
With day and night and day and night and
Nature must go by the way.

Black pillars for those beauteous trees,
Man gives nature this grave sight
Of death, destruction, and of blight.
And death and death and death and death
Of nature, goodness, and of ... **MAN.**

When man is under graves of earth,
The country will be quiet and still.
The trees have leaves,
The grass and hill
Do not make a noisy sound,
When men are underneath the ground.

HIS POEMS
The Toy

When I was just a little boy,
A sweet five years of age,
My mother gave me a gun, a toy
Of plastic; it made a clicking sound
At which you ought to ... all fall down,
But always to get up again.

It never let you drown
In anguish, sweat, and dirt,
And blood ... and what's the word?
For it couldn't kill or hurt
A man, a child or boy
For though it looked so real
It yet was but a toy.

When I was eighteen years of age,
As innocent as a child,
My people gave me a toy
And warned me it was wild.
But I did not understand
What it could do to boy and man.
It made a funny clicking sound.

They did not rise up from the ground,
For the ketchup was too red,
The mess of gut and blood and dead.
Dead that's it, the word is dead.
The bloody frozen muck of flesh lying there so quiet
and – dead.
I was crying as I saw,
I'll hear that clicking sound no more,
For men must learn to get no joy,
From playing with this deadly toy.

DAVID

Tin Soldiers

Little tin soldiers,
Standing in a row.
Left right, left right,
Up and down they go.
Sergeant giving orders,
Booming with a will.
Fourteen-year-old soldier boys,
Learning how to kill.

Violence breeds more violence,
Monday afternoon,
Regimented soldier boys,
Learning war too soon.
Wearing pretty uniforms,
Duty to the flag.
Belt and buckles shining.
Don't let your spirits sag.

Standing there like robots,
You must not think at all.
Thought is a grievous crime,
Just hear the sergeant's call.
Good for moral fibre?
Is it really so,
When you're taught not to think,
How can your minds grow?

Parading there so smartly,
Standing there so still,
Fourteen-year-old soldier boys,
Learning how to kill.

HIS POEMS

Drought

The people ask for rain,
The children pray for rain,
Old women cry for rain,
And yet it does not come.

The heat is getting worse
The maddening heat and dirt
And yet it does not come.

The crops they brown and die
Cow's bones show through their thigh
Men in hell's dirt do lie
And yet it does not come.

The villages are in dust
A death has come that must
Make great India bust
And yet it does not come.

CREATIVE TALENT – PAINTINGS

Marek Zulawski

Son of an eminent Polish author, born in Rome, educated at the Warsaw Academy of Fine Art and in Paris, Marek Zulawski lived and painted in London from 1937 until his death in 1985.

His work has been exhibited extensively in Britain and Europe, and is included in collections in leading museums and art galleries on both sides of the Atlantic.

For many years he broadcast on art in Britain for the BBC while his books have a significant place in art criticism, particularly on the continent of Europe.

He has been described as 'an artist of stature whose paintings speak to us of the drama of contemporary human existence'.

DAVID

Appreciation

It is a well-known fact that children produce most enchanting paintings simply because they spontaneously give expression to the primordial creative instinct of the species – and hardly ever anything else. They cannot go wrong because instinct never goes wrong. It is the intellect that is prone to errors, the errors of judgement and the errors of taste acquired in an environment from the grown-ups. Children very rarely continue painting when they become adolescents and their creative instinct ceases to drive them. That period of life begins with a birth of awkwardness, doubt and intellectual self-consciousness. Consequently, paintings by teenagers are mediocre and hesitant as a rule, even though their work might have been delightful when they were children.

David was an exception to this rule as to many others, and the most unusual fact about his art is that these designs and paintings which he left are most interesting.

He did not start to paint in any coherent way until he became seriously ill which happened at the age of 20 in 1977, and all his important work was done whilst confined to bed after that. It was a short burst of frantic creative activity. He died in July 1978.

David's work could be divided into two clear categories. There are some – very few in fact – representational paintings which perhaps, could be treated as illustrations to his poems. They are very expressionist – just like his poems – but rather subdued in colour.

The second category, which forms the bulk of his work and is by far the more interesting from a purely visual point of view, is completely non-representational. Here belong

CREATIVE TALENT – PAINTINGS

designs of geometric character, reminiscent of some Buddhist Mandalas – perhaps inspired by some esoteric philosophical ideas, but certain, in my opinion – valid primarily as unusual patterns of great beauty. Those geometrical puzzles spreading all over the sheet of paper in an organic or crystalline sort of way are most violently coloured, in strange harmonies and juxtapositions. They are also completely two dimensional in concept.

Some of them remind me of Paul Klee. Taken together they form a body of work that could be shown in any contemporary art gallery. They radiate their peculiar individuality, at the same time brilliantly decorative and mysterious. One can visualise these paintings as concomitant with some future Beings belonging to the space fictions that were favourite reading matter of the young man.

It would be tempting to speculate on the potential possibilities of such art form, should the artist have been given the chance to evolve it on a larger scale as mural decorations or tapestries.

CREATIVE TALENT – MUSIC

Bert Weedon

Born in London, Bert Weedon was one of the best-known popular guitarists in Britain. Trained in the classical guitar, his career had been a notable success in the field of jazz, rock, dance and other forms of popular music.

He was celebrated as a concert soloist, accompanist, and performer in many parts of the world, and appeared in over 5,000 radio and television shows. He received numerous coveted awards, not only as a performer, but also as a composer, and on nine occasions was voted Britain's leading popular music guitarist.

Known also as 'the man who taught the world to play the guitar', his guitar tutor *Play in a Day* sold over a million copies. He was an acknowledged authority on the guitar throughout the world.

CREATIVE TALENT – MUSIC

Appreciation

In his comments on David's paintings, Marek Zulawski says that children produce enchanting paintings giving expression to the primordial creative instincts, but that they rarely continue painting when they become adolescents and teenagers. I think that this is true, but the situation is reversed in the art of music. It is when they become teenagers that so many young people enter the world of music, and in particular the world of popular music, creating their own styles and forms of expression.

David, whom I never had the pleasure of meeting, entered the world of music as a teenager, and spent more and more of his last few years playing the guitar. His father, Aubrey, whom I met after David's passing, let me hear the recorded tapes that David's brother made at home of David's playing. The music he created represents so clearly the drive, energy and frustrations of his generation. Through it we hear many things – the reaction of a sensitive, thinking, young man to the world about him – a world that is sadly uncertain, violent, and in a state of confused, changing values and the struggles of many people for new values in society.

His rhythms, aggressive and strident, are the sounds that so many young people find express their own feelings. Then the music changes to long passages of solo guitar playing that show a great depth of emotion and passion – the music of a young man pouring out his heart into florid musical phrases. His style incorporates the 'blues' of the American negroes, and the passion and intensity of his Jewish background, for his race have contributed so much to the world of music, and David is a true exponent of all the depth of sadness and yet eternal hope and vitality of his people – a music that is ever-hopeful and virile and yet conveys the sadness of the past.

I understand that David was mainly self-taught, apart from some early rudimentary instruction, and I am amazed at his dexterity as a performer. His flights of melodic invention are so adventurous and promising; could it be that he was trying to say so much in his music before he died?

I am certain that David would have made a big impression in the popular music world had fate given him more time to develop his ideas and emotions. Sadly, we are left only with the sounds of his early ideas on home-recorded tapes, but I am sure that given the facilities of ideal recording techniques and a top-rate instrument, David would have achieved a highly respected place in the world of popular music.

With his paintings, poems, and music, David has left something for us to think about. I only wish I had known him – he had so much to say; he has surely left his mark forever.

CREATIVE TALENT – MUSIC

His Lyrics

In his Appreciation, Bert Weedon comments on David's musical composition and performance, while George Lamming refers to the growing social awareness in the *lyrics*. I would add a short note of explanation.

I have included ten of the songs David wrote in the summer of 1977, which I feel to be the most representative.

In all of them the words are subordinate to the rhythm and melody, words and short phrases oft-repeated, frequently impressionistic and 'atmospheric', dwelling in the half-light between prose and poetry.

The song 'Carnival' alludes to the West Indian-inspired Carnival, held annually in the streets of West London, which, in 1977, unhappily became the scene of conflict.

In 'Big Game Hunter' the words are wholly conditioned by the strong, stirring rhythm of the music.

The others explain themselves, although a few have a kind of mystery that perhaps only David can explain.

DAVID

Man from the Ministry

See the man, with the gun in his hand,
Tired, yet alert all the while.
See the hate and the humour there
See the cold burning smile.

He lived for himself and the wet drips of death
He lived for excitement and thrills.
He lived to see fear in the eyes of men
That he never 'really' wanted to kill.

He was born in a bad part of Hampstead
Where he grew up to be a great power
He lived his whole life in business and strife,
And killed with his pen every hour.

In the morning he shines of cold lightning,
His car it burns down the road.
But what can he do, to me or to you
Depends on the power that you hold.

The power
To hold on to the gold to be bold.
To hold on to the gold to be bold.
To be told to be bold, to be told to be bold
To be bold for the man from the Ministry

CREATIVE TALENT – MUSIC

City

Here I live my life just for today
Know tonight where I can find a lay
Know it's here that I am going to stay
Here, in the heart of the city.

People moving, things to do all night
Happy neon, flashing till the light
Little girls playing in my sight
Here, in the heart of the city.

(Chorus)
Sometimes, when I'm tired
And I feel uninspired
It's so cold in the heart of the city.

There are times in the night,
When I feel I just might,
Be better off outside of the city.
Want to play around and have some fun,
Don't want to be the only lonely one
Want to keep on moving till the sun,
Here, in the heart of the city.

DAVID

Silvren Lady

Sunshine, in her eyes
Flickering gently, flickering bright

Stardust, in her smile,
Spreading sweet magic all the while

Moonlight, floating in gold
A single strand of her hair, it glows

She's a Lady, Silvren you see
Burnished amber, she'll set you free.

Silvren lady, silvren child
Come to me gently, come to me wild.

CREATIVE TALENT – MUSIC

Chess

The black magician sits playing boisterous games,
Juggling with the feelings of the ladies that he tames,
Smoothing curving pathways through their gently tear-stained dreams
Strumming on their beings, composing one note themes.

The red queen, she lays tin soldiers on her board
Standing them in ranks, stacking them in drawers
Leaves them dead and dripping, drying in the sun,
Laughs at the crippled images as she grabs another one.

Pawns spinning, turning circles
Caught in the spiralling net,
Endings never lead to dawn
Beginnings to sunset.

Magician and the red Queen, sit in the lighted Hall
Moving knights and bishops adroitly round the floor
Who in turn string their puppets, gaily painted dancers
Who sing and ask their questions, but never find the answers.

The blue king in his castle lets all his mirrors spin,
He daubs them with a paintbrush as the images begin,
He controls the red and silver, he knows the secret way
But now he finds he cannot stop his blue from turning grey.

DAVID

Drifting

When the river flows past my door
The crowds all call on me for more
I don't follow the road or the sky
I see the fires burning in their eye.

Green meadows roll on by
Gently till the time it comes to die
I wake each day, still to see the sun
Lazily I watch the passing fun.

(Chorus)
I don't need to follow
I just sit right down
Tomorrow when it comes will be tomorrow
I'll still be around.

A drifter to you I may seem
A child lost in a dream
But I rarely need to cry
Don't see such sadness in my eye.

CREATIVE TALENT – MUSIC

Franki and Jenny

Jenny was a lady out of school,
Had to work each day to keep fed,
Her parents and her teachers taught her rules,
Now she spends most of her time in bed.
Keep on, keep on, working.

Franki was guy with some ambitions,
Aimed to own a lot of human flesh,
Destroyed all young Jenny's inhibitions,
Crippled here in his powerful silken mesh.
Keep on, keep on, selling.

Jenny didn't like her work.
Greasy stench, the squalid dirt,
Needed Franki just to keep her sane,
Franki gave her lots of love,
A place to sleep, sometimes enough,
But he used her just the same.

Jenny learnt the tricks of her profession,
Could make her clients come in lots of ways,
But she lost all pleasure in the sessions,
Was hard as nails and dead in all but name.
Keep on, keep on, earning.

DAVID

The Pattener

The seven Isles knew his fame,
Kings and Princes to him came,
None of them were quite the same,
They didn't understand his game,
They never learnt his name.

Power over words he had,
Power over deeds of man,
Kept the circle in his hand,
Saw to it that stillness ruled the land,
Life he formed out of a grain of sand.

Secretly he passed his years,
Living with no need of fear,
Secure in power was he here,
Until the thought of his death did appear,
Crisp upon the glass were his tears.

Death it came, it called his name.
The Pattener he had to change,
For all in all he was the same,
As all the cowering peasants that he spurned,
Yet here was something that he had not learned.

CREATIVE TALENT – MUSIC

Carnival

Hustled violence
In the street
People swarm
Frightened meat
Blood and shit
In pools around
Trampled bodies
On the ground.

What a day for a fine procession
Sunshine, dancing, games and no depression.

The battle comes
The sunshine goes
Broken bottles
Rubber hose
People all
Having fun
Kicking the shit
Out of someone.

Except the ones, who come for quieter pleasures
Who tried to make a happy day of leisure
But saw their hopes end in battle dust
As children clashed with coppers, as they must.

DAVID

Big Game Hunter

Come down to the town
Looking for adventure
Gonna find something to do
Find a little girl
Have a little pleasure
We ain't nothing to lose

(Chorus)
I'm a big game hunter
I'm after wild cats' hides
I'm a big game hunter
I don't spare no lives

I've been round the world
Gun upon my shoulder
I've got to get away from you
Haven't the heart
To stay here any longer
Doing what I have to do

Don't mess around, with no brown sugar
Don't need no painted halls
Don't need no saviour, don't need no pusher
Got me trophies on the wall

CREATIVE TALENT – MUSIC

Young Love

See my baby, see my lady
Walking down the street
She looks so young, looks so fine
Looks so good to me
Gently as she's lying
She whispers out my name
Talking in a silent voice
A wave on me she breaks.

Together we will travel
A road to find the sun
Searching for it, seeking it
Our love will reach out on.
I don't know, and I can't say
What she has done for me
All I know, all I feel
Is she has set me free.

I will fight to hold on to my love – on to my love.

TALKS

During the 1990s, I was privileged to be able to deliver a series of talk on the BBC World Service. These talks referred to David in various ways, and I reproduce the texts of two the talks here.

DAVID

1st Talk – BBC World Service

The Blackbird

A young seven-year-old looks out at what is around him, sits down, and writes a poem. It is about a bird. Listen to the young poet.

The Blackbird

*A Blackbird sitting in a tree
Sings his song of melody
He sings his song, so loud and clear
So all the people round can hear.*

*But the people hurrying by
Do not hear the bird on high
They are too busy with other things
To hear the song the blackbird sings*

*But the blackbird does not care
About the people hurrying there
He sings his song himself to please
Sitting there amongst the trees.*

Has this seven-year-old recognised something we older people often miss? We get up, go to earn a living, provide food, shelter and clothing. In the great cities how often are we 'too busy with other things' seeing to the household, travelling to and from work, immersed in daily affairs. We are the children of the modern age, of wonders, grasping at every new technical invention, often surrounding ourselves with noise.

In the last century Charles Darwin announced his theory of the evolution of the species, one form of life developing out of a previous form, better adapted to survive. Today he might have come forward with a theory of the evolution of the technical species.

First, we had the telegraph, then the telephone, followed by the telex, replaced by the fax, itself followed by email, surfing eventually into the all-encompassing Internet, leaving aside the miracles of radio and television. Who knows what comes next?

Yet all these wonderful machines are witness to *how* we communicate, not *what* we communicate.

The great teachers of old didn't need them, yet their messages have not changed. Moses, Jesus, Mahomet, Buddha, the great holy men of India, they did not need these modern wonders.

They went out into the silence of the desert, climbed a remote mountain, sat still under a tree. They were not 'too busy with other things' to hear the song that came to them from across time and space. Around them people were hurrying by, caught up in a whirlpool of activity immersed in a fog of many sounds, hearing nothing. The great teachers though heard the song of melody, the song of truth that came to them 'so loud and clear' that they try their utmost to pass on their message of hope.

Throughout man's history, so brief compared to endless time, blackbirds have sung their wonderful songs, and so often we, ordinary people as the young poet says, are 'too busy with other things to hear the song the blackbird sings'.

DAVID

As for me, I get a glimmer of the universal melody only in the early morning as the darker night slowly gives way to the soft morning light when all around me are asleep, people, machines, everything and I look out onto the grass and trees and listen. If I really listen, truly listen, sometimes I hear the song of the blackbird before the sun rises and before the world, the busy world around me, starts yet another day.

Whether we hear his voice or not, the blackbird is always near us, sitting there among the trees. He has been there for years. If we really try, we might just hear him before the daily blanket of noise descends on us. It needs an effort, but it is worth it. Who knows what may happen to you, if one day, you hear a voice or melody you never heard before.

TALKS

2nd Talk - BBC World Service

Drought

My son David died of cancer when he was aged 21. Until then he was a prolific poet. I re-read one of his poems the other day, a poem he wrote when he was 13. It's called 'Drought'. Listen to this short poem.

Drought

The people ask for rain,
The children pray for rain,
Old women cry for rain
And yet it does not come.

The heat is getting worse
The maddening heat and dirt,
And yet it does not come.

The crops they brown and die
Cow's bones show through their thigh
Men in hell's dirt do lie
And yet it does not come.

The villages are in dust
A death has come that must
Make great India bust
And yet it does not come.

Only those who live in parts of the world where the coming of the rains means life and where their failure means hunger, famine, death, can truly appreciate what drought means.

In Britain, Europe, parts of the Western hemisphere, we sometimes joke about the rain, make it a topic of polite conversation. In some places the rains pour down incessantly, in torrents, from which one needs protection.

But there are parts of the world, especially in Africa, in Asia, on the edge of deserts, on soil-cracked plains, where people depend upon water from above for their very lives.

In this poem we sense the pain of these millions in India. *'The people **ask** for rain, the children **pray** for rain, old women **cry** for rain, and yet it does not come'.* They were desperate. Man must have bread first to be able then to develop his other gifts.

There have been famines in the past. The scriptures tell of them. Modern peoples, the Irish for example, can tell of the consequences. Drought has hit the heart of the United States in past years just as today it afflicts Sudan and other lands of Africa.

We need water to live. Our bodies are 80% water. The surface of our planet is two-thirds water. We build dams, sink wells, deepen rivers, to assure ourselves of sufficient water. The richer nations try to help the poorer, as they should, until the poorer peoples can help themselves. That is why experiments to make the desert bloom, to prevent topsoil disappearing, are so important, why science is so important.

Yet suddenly there can sometimes be too much water. Think of the people of Bangladesh whose homes, and indeed whose lives, have been swept away in recent months by massive floods, caused not only by the monsoons, but also by man's destruction of forests higher up the river valley, sweeping away the topsoil and causing havoc hundreds of miles away. No nation is an island.

Water too has been a symbol in our great religions, ceremonial washing, immersion in rivers, cleaning bodies, clean hands, the washing away of sins, living waters. Drought in the land can also accompany drought in the soul, in the mind, in the heart, a drying-up of goodness and moral feeling. How well does the first Psalm in the Bible describe the righteous man, *'He shall be like a tree planted by streams of water. That bringeth forth its fruit in its season. And whose leaves do not wither'.* May we all be spared from the drought within us and the drought around us.

David had an unusual gift of moral perception as happens with other young poets of sensitivity. Later, lying on his bed, the last bed he would lie on, he urged me to send money to relieve famine in India. Though unaffected himself by famine, he shared in the suffering of those who were and who prayed for rain. To share the feelings and sufferings of others, and to do something about it, remains a constant challenge to each and every one of us.

In 1987, for the first time, we had confirmation from David himself of the significance of the colours and shapes. Leslie Flint, who had been faithfully assisted in much of his career by his secretary, Bram Rogers, came one bright May day to our home with Bram and others in the small group, and held a sitting in our dining room. The old, original, wooden shutters of the house came into practical use, possibly for the first time this century, in helping to keep out the sunlight.

David was delighted with the way his mother had reproduced his drawings in tapestry and needlework. *'Better than my originals,'* he commented. He went on at some length to explain the origin of his designs:

> *'In their own way the pictures had meaning. Each motif represents experiences.*
>
> *When I was lying there my mind was transported, received visions and imprints. I tried to recreate things. They represent more than they seem. Each part represents aspects of emotion and feeling, not just myself. This is a link.*
>
> *They are symbolic to a point, but represent individuals, emotions. I realise now someone was guiding me. I have met people here who were creative and artistic in their own time. I was much influenced by Barney. There is a collective harmony. They tell a story, there is much more to it than meets the eye. I didn't know it at the time. I knew I didn't have long to stay with you. The way was being prepared for me. I was doing that to express things I didn't understand.*
>
> *Since I've been here, I've met people and understand they were utilising me in a special way.*
>
> *I love you. I shall always be behind you, every step of the way. There are people here you never mentioned. We are a much bigger, wider family. We are all one. I shall remain for a long time the individual as you remember me, although I shall be on a much different level in some respects.*

People are being prepared. We are never alone. In the nights, when I didn't sleep, I was not alone. Nothing can separate us. We are much bigger than we seem. I knew that I had a death warrant. It didn't worry me. I was worried about you. The things I might have done I can do here. Everything here is much more real than you will ever know.

We are like brothers and sisters, much more than that. We are not that far away as you may think. Time for us is not as it is for you. We are a family, a much bigger family than you can imagine. Some have been here for centuries. Never grieve for me. I love you.'

David's words flowed clearly, unhesitatingly, with such a sense of affection and attachment. I reproduce here only extracts. He was now here with us at home, not merely a sense of his presence, but his very words. We detected the faintest wistfulness at his not being here physically too. But we knew the strength of the link that could never be broken, providing a confidence and an assurance that has sustained me ever since his death, and has enabled me to cope with his passing from us.

ARTEFACTS

I present here a small number of items, relating to public viewings of David's work, in 1984, and to a commemorative event celebrating David's life, in 1996.

The Old Bull events, in 1984, were supplemented by a veritable host of great speakers, including Dame Cicely Saunders, founder of the hospice movement, cancer research experts Jack Kusick and Roger King, and notable artists Edward Blishen, writer, John Thompson, painter, and sculptor John Somerville.

DAVID ROSE

1957-1978

paintings · poems · drawings

Exhibition & Lectures

till 18 Feb

Saturday 4th February	'HOSPICE EVOLUTION' by DAME CICELY SAUNDERS, DBE, FRCP Medical Director of St Christophers' Hospice, London SE20 and leading figure in the Hospice Movement 2.30pm
Thursday 9th February	'PROBLEMS AND PROGRESS IN CANCER RESEARCH' A Symposium led by leading research experts from the Imperial Cancer Research Fund. Dr JACK CUSICK and Dr R.J.B.KING 8pm
Saturday 11th February	'CREATING ART' A panel of leading local artists will describe their own artistic experiences and development. Those participating include EDWARD BLISHEN (writer), JOHN M THOMPSON (painter) and JOHN SOMERVILLE (sculptor)

All proceeds to

The OLD BULL DEVELOPMENT TRUST
and IMPERIAL CANCER RESEARCH FUND

OLD BULL
GALLERY & THEATRE

68 High Street, Barnet
449.0048

A Brush with Eternity
THE CREATIVE SPIRIT
A talk by Aubrey Rose OBE

The Spiro Institute is delighted to invite you to a talk by Aubrey Rose, author of 'Journey Into Immortality' which he wrote to commemorate the extraordinary creative artistic genius his son David displayed in the face of affliction and tragic death at 21 years of age.

David Colman Rose was born in London on 30th January 1957. He attended City of London School and studied law at Leeds University and Queen Mary's College, London. He was a keen sportsman and musician until the onset of his illness. He died in London on 5th July 1978.

"David Rose, an extraordinary person who deserves to be very widely known. His story while inevitably sad, is also life enhancing. If this is the quality of which human beings may be made, than humanity is indeed worth saving." Martyn Goff OBE

**SUNDAY 12TH MAY 1996 AT 7.30 PM
ROOM 6. THE SPIRO INSTITUTE
C/O KING'S COLLEGE LONDON
KIDDERPORE AVENUE, NW3
ENTRANCE: £5 INCLUDING RECEPTION**
For tickets and information please telephone 0171 431 0345

AUBREY ROSE OBE is Senior Vice-President of the Board of Deputies of British Jews, former Deputy Chairman, Commission for Racial Equality, founder member of the Commonwealth Human Rights Initiative and author of Judaism and Ecology, Jewish Communities of the Commonwealth, and Brief Encounters of a Legal Kind, a review of causes and cases in his legal career.

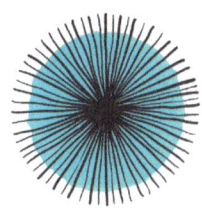

TAPESTRIES

Many of David's most colourful paintings were emulated in tapestry form by my beloved wife, Sheila. They continue to adorn my house to this day ... and are very much admired.

From David

www.ingramcontent.com/pod-product-compliance
Lightning Source LLC
LaVergne TN
LVHW051226070526
838200LV00057B/4624